Love, Peace and
Sweet Tea

LLB Publishing House
Los Angeles, California
eMail: leezalee7@yahoo.com

First Printing: March 2022
10 9 8 7 6 5 4 3 2 1

ISBN: 979-8-9852026-0-1 (paperback)

ISBN: 979-8-9852026-1-8 (hardcover)

ISBN: 979-8-9852026-2-5 (eBook)

Love, Peace and Sweet Tea

A Collection Of Poetry And A
Compelling Short Story

LEEZA LEE BARR

In loving memory of my mother
Lavern Person Lott

who inspired me to write poetry.
She would be proud to know
that I followed in her footsteps.
RIP.

Acknowledgment

First and foremost, to God, for guiding my hands
Ricarlo Porter, circuit promoter and friend
Janet Marcelin, contributing editor and mentor
My three sons, Mark Anthony Lott, Michael
Lott (deceased), and Brian Fields.
Also all my family, including play daughter Kimberly
Raymond and lifelong friend Etta-McCardell.

God Bless Leezalee with her words of enlightenment. She touches hope and the spirit of truth. For God has formed her to be a blessing through her poetry. Let this book be inspiration to all who believe in Love, Peace and Sweet Tea.

Dr. Amos J. Young Sr., Pastor

Leezalee sees love as the driving force in life. Her insight is evident in her writing. The enthusiasm with which she shares her thought is prose and in poetry can lighten the spirit and bring joy to the heart.

Gwendolyn Reed J.D.
Educator, Author

My Poems

My poems are love.
They're about healing
They'll turn your frown into a smile.
They create mental files.
Bring forth joy and happiness like the heart of a child.
Go ahead, connect with your spirituality.
They may even change your functionality.
I hope you feel as I do.
Take the time to listen.
My poems convey life, forgiveness, redemption, and
Hope to all folks.

My poems are love, peace, and sweet tea.
My poems are full of life, happy, and free.
They want to heal the heart.
We all deserve a new start.

Like the sweet smell of jasmine, orange
blossoms, and cherries paired—
My poems sing to the soul.
They'll never turn their back on you.
My poems are God's love; it's true!

CONTENTS

SECTION 3
Sweet Tea

SECTION 6

Romance

A COMPELLING SHORT STORY

Empress of the Fringes

Section 1
Love

Love Tree

From all things a root must they start.
This grows, develops, and forms the base.
Ever growing, expanding, spreading,
Branching to all those whom we touch.

Limbs are formed with beautiful leaves.
Sprouting the beginnings of love, my love tree.

The buds open and bloom.
The aroma of jasmine flirts through the air,
Spreading to all showing its love.
Continually growing into maturity,
Like love between you and me.

Living, breathing, and bringing joy to each heart till eternity.
Love tree for you and me.

I Know Love

Love is colorless.
Boundless.
Love has feeling.
It heals the mind.
It penetrates every cell.

Plato's cave couldn't bound love.
Cupid, his arrows boundless.
Love renews and shapes us.
The love of God; it carries me.
Without it, I am lost.
It takes me to the ends of the earth.
Lifts me up ever higher.
My hope, I know love.

Love Is

Love is the master key to all things.
Honesty and trust are essential for love to open things up.
A divine gift.
Love defines each heart.
Reads like a novel.
Have you ever heard of the book of love?

Love has a master's degree; it lectures on high.
Love is the master key to one's heart.
A combination of honesty and devotion
is essential for a beautiful start.
It's difficult to define.
It's an incredible joy to love and be loved.

Love is never having to say goodbye.
It can bring tears to your eyes like falling rain.
Love has no limits.
It cannot be measured no matter how hard you try.

You can't get around love.
It reaches the lowest lows and the highest highs.
For Love is God and God is Love.

Treasured Love

Love is a marvelous thing,
It's better when savored, rather than a passion fling.

Someone who truly loves is rare.
Love is always present, always constant, always there.

Don't be fooled by beauty or style.
Beauty is only skin deep that last for a while.

Love is more valuable than shimmery gold,
To be pleasured and treasured, not bartered or sold.

To find love is exciting and thrilling.
It's a marvelous adventure when there's mutual feelings.

To find love is a valued treasure,
It's bountiful and something you cannot measure.

Love Is the Motivator

Love is the motivator,
It's a gift from the creator.
It's the core of what makes me tick.
Waking up early, taking a shower,
Love is the best lipstick.

Having my morning tea, I feel blessed,
Beaming with joy as I get dressed.
Thinking of a new love I can't wait to see
While sipping on my spiced sweet tea.

I feel blessed to know love.
I like to think like love.
Love is my pub, my check stub,
My bathtub.
Love is sweet tea.
Love gives me a raise every day.
What a motivator!

Love and Peace

Love, Peace, and Sweet Tea

Love, peace, and sweet tea.
Tea soothes like love.
Peace flows like tea.
Love parts red seas!
Love tastes sweet like honey.

Bees sing about the sweetness,
The happiness of love, peace, and sweet tea.
They taste good together.

God's love flows in the peace and calm of living waters.
God's love flows in sweetness.
Soothes the mind, body, and soul.
Frees the mind, body, and soul.
Healing!

Friends Forever

We have a long track record
Longer than the railroad tracks
We go way back

Call me no matter what for
I will always be at the door
Weather bad or fair
I will always be there

My care is like a freight train
It gets to where you are again and again
It doesn't matter the distance
Just remember we are friends forever

Love, Don't Let It Go

Love . . . you are blessed like the angel Gabriel.
Shining like a morning star.
It reaches all earth.

Amazing gifts flowing from agape love.
Like butterflies these gifts are amazing.
Love, don't let it go.

Love Is Amazing

Love nourishes us.
It helps us grow.
So what's the fuss?
Let love grow in your heart.
Start a love garden.
See your fruit there.
Love is amazing, amazing is love.

Finding Love

To find love, don't look very far.
It starts with you wherever you are.

Just look inside, let love through,
Then you'll see the real you.

Love doesn't turn blue,
No matter what you do.
It has no color,
Yet it is colorful.

Love is amazing, so amazing.
Savor it,
Don't let it go,
Make it last.
We are amazing
Because of love, you are!

SECTION 2
Peace

At Sunset

At sunset, I sit by the ocean.
I watch the motion of the waves roll in.
I'm at peace with myself at the day's end.

At sunset I feel the cool breeze across my face.
Calmness and serenity I embrace.
I watch the sun descend from an orange glazed sky.
To worries I'm saying goodbye.

I can live forever now and kiss bliss . . . at sunset.

Let It Rain

Listen to the sound of the rain against my window pane.
I look out in the night,
Raindrops roll down.
Raindrops dance on the ground.
Stuff keeps crashing down.
How can I turn things around?

I must dance like the rain to escape my pain.
Let it rain!
It makes me feel free again.
Let it rain,
I can dance like the rain.
I'll be Fred Astaire, instead of in despair.
Let it rain!

Going Home Blues

I've been gone so long.
I believe I'll go back home.
I've got to find my baby and unite my happy home.

I'm going home to my nest
High up, high up in my family's tree.
That's where I want to be.

I went to Hollywood, had my name in lines.
I was a star. I made it to the top.
My fame was destroyed by drugs, women, and wine.

Now, I believe, I believe I'll go back home.
I've got to find my baby; that's where I belong.
Back down home—where I belong.
No more will I roam.

Come and go with me—to my family tree.

Slipped Away

Nine scores and five, you beautiful butterfly.
You've blessed lives like they were flowers in the cold.
I miss you like a rainbow after a great downpour.
You loved hand to bottom, heart to soul.
Butterfly, butterfly, butterfly!

I cried raindrops, thunder, and lightning.
You slipped away just twenty minutes into a new day.
Just moments into infinity.
Just a step before paradise . . . butterfly!

Let the color of your wings lift up my days.
Let your wings open the sky.

Lavern Lott was here
And shall always be . . .
A butterfly!

Departed

Your voice is silent,
You can see my smile.
Angel at my side
You have free miles.

Like a dove you can fly,
Transcend higher highs.
You're in a better place now.
Free from the pounds, free to let go.
Free to embrace the flow.

I know you love me.
You will always be a part of me.
Here in my heart, true soldiers never depart.
I treasure the memories.
I see your flag, your spark.
Your clothes still sharp.
The miracles we shared.
For this trip, you were prepared.

Walking in the Rain

At midnight, I go out in the rain.
Feeling the heartache and pain.
Rain drops, falling on my face,
I walked by our favorite place.
I'm missing you, your smile,
Laughter and sweet embrace.

Tears begin to roll down from my eyes onto my cheeks.
There, the rain and my tears meet.
I feel the emptiness and loss.
I need you back in my life at any cost!

I'm walking in the rain,
I feel the pain of losing you.
What can I do?
This heart aches for you.

My heart will heal in time.
Therefore, I ignore the blurry signs.
Gradually, it soothes my heartache and pain.
Till I mend I contend to walk in the rain.

Morning Glory

Can you see the morning glory?
Another day of beauty tells a story.
Blossoms and trees, blue birds and bliss.
A new day springs forth like a leap frog seeking a kiss.
We walk in God's grace.

A white flower in full bloom brightens June.
The smell of rain in the air.
A rainbow in Martinique: laughing cheek to cheek
Morning glory.

A new day springs forth.
Morning glory awakens joy and humble spirits.
Budding trees in the spring, blue birds
coo and sing; of morning glory.
Another day of beauty tells the story of God's grace.

Quietness

This house whispers of you.
The subtle signs that you were once here,
The little things you use to do.

The art on the wall of Billy Holiday and the Duke.
Hearkens me back to our youth.
I miss the sound of your footsteps; the sad distant echoes.
This house hushes without you.
Those old jazz records you use to play, now missing from my days.

It's too quiet in here!

I Cried

My last tear over you.
My eyes dry, they pour no more drinks.
My last tears over you.
Now my time won't miss a clear blink.
My heart pours out into the blue.
I cried my last tear over you.

I have a new path now.
Don't hurt anymore,
Heartbreak took a flight,
I'm blessed.
I'm all right.
I cried my last tear over you.

SECTION 3
Sweet Tea

On Mother's Day

Families travel the weekend; blissful reunions abound.
It's Mother's Day once again.
The streets and stores are jammed.
Baskets are filled with perfume, flowers, and balloons.
Kids are playing in the yard, they made mom a card.
Kitchens everywhere smell of turkey, hot wings, and ham.
Family members bring potato salad.
It just makes the occasion seem so valid.

Kinfolks gather around in their Sunday best.
Smiles on everyone's faces taking their places.
Mom says grace, Uncle Joe says, "Let's eat!"
These treasured moments just can't be beat
On Mother's Day.

Sisters with Attitude

Sisters with attitude are super.
Sisters with attitude are superb.
Sisters are passionate about their bucks
About music, about learning.
They're like a yellow bus rolling.
They're like pillars in Rome.

Sisters with attitude carry a nation,
Carry a message, carry love.
They're like a jet plane.
They're like Lisa and Sheryl,
Venus and Serena.

Doors are opening, many doors.
Bridges are being crossed.
These sisters are boss.
Diana Ross would be proud
To stand by these champions
They won't be denied
Somebody testify!
Sisters with attitude
Have something to say
It's time for brothas to
Help them bring in a brighter day.

Sister, Sistah

What you possess forms worlds.
Solar systems.
What you possess, Ike can't break;
Tina can't lose.
Young girls can use.
Queen of African nations.
Child of God's soul.
Precious priceless bloodline
Gold and diamond flesh.
What you possess is beauty and God's grace.
It's written all over your face.

Take it Off

Take it all off
The layers of lies, deceit, and pride
The anger and the abuse
Take it off

Hey, phantom, end your opera
Unveil the real
Hey, you in Congress
Stop the gridlock
Put on some Jesus

Take off the stress and duress
Take it off like makeup
Take off the worry
Put on some glory
Take off the frown
Put on a smile

Hey, relatives take off the fighting and jealousy
Take it off like dirty clothes
And when you take it off . . .
Don't put that junk back on

This Country

This country is a fat cat;
You can see it on the news.
Meanwhile, my kids walk to school
With holes in their shoes.
Corruption, inflation.
What's happen to our nation?
Uncle Sam claims he's broke
But keeps giving to the rich folk.

Oh, thank God!
I know how to pray.
Now, my kids have new shoes
And I'm feeling okay.

Is Freedom Ringing?

Am I free to be all I can be?
Or am I chained to a tree?
Do I fulfill the potential God has set for me?
Am I free to touch the sky or to sail the sea?
My mind and soul are free.
My body has a loose chain around it,
So I don't go too far. Deal with it!
I made a change.
I broke that chain.
I'm free to be me,
To teach love to my offspring.
Love is king.
Ring like blue birds sing.
Break the loose chain!
Break out,
Break loose.
Break free.
Free of worry and doom.
Free as the sun and moon.
Let your bells ring!

My Country

Young, slave babies, cried, "Let Freedom Ride."
The robbery of mothers and fathers died.
The dry bones, now wet, with sea water.
Cry out, to my ears, for this country's passion and fears.
My poetry, my music, takes me to a place
and across roads on the way.

My country, now there's a tree, without leaves.
Standing alone, in the nude, and being treated rude.
Real estate under fine rule.

My country fears of thee,
Handcuffed and wearing a frown,
Drunk on the way to jail.
My country's love for sale, on the auction block.

How can I love you when you wouldn't love me back?
Just like a deck of cards, the dealer got the whole stack.
My people, my country.

The Mask

I can see through it,
How phony can you be?
I'm not fooled by your smooth talk
Or jazzy walk.
Take off the layers of viciousness and hate.
Your true self is revealed,
Through your eyes and fake smile.
The mask says it all,
Yet you hide behind it.
I can see through you,
Reveal yourself,
Stop the pretense of being someone else.
Your true character has shown its face,
Beguile, corrupt,
From a secret place you deceive many,
Take it off.
I see who you really are.
Take off the layers of meanness and hate;
Where's the little angel?
The mask tells a lie.
Take off those years of mistrust.
Take off the finger pointing.
Take it off!

Dem City Folks

Dem' folks came from the city.
Dressed in their Sunday best.
Don't they look pretty
Struttin' round, looking fresh.
Women excuse themselves to powder their noses.

I wish I had their style,
But Mama says I'm still a child.
I'd like to wear powder, rouge, and paint,
Sexy skirts and pants with style.

Mama says go with your dad
And pick some cotton
While I wish I could dance a few steps of the Black Bottom.
Other girls are spoiled rotten.

I left but quickly turn to see,
Dem' city folk doing the Bumble Bee.
They danced and pranced around.
I didn't know Mama could get down.

They continued to dance.
Some men told jokes
Drinking and having a ball
Instead I must work in the cotton fields.
I don't know what to feel.

September, Remember!

September, remember the colored leaves,
The trees and yellow buses.
Couples kissing near their bikes.
Children playing, laughing
Church singing, bells ringing.
Remember the good times,
Flipping, dancing, swinging.
Remember the big love?
The fights we got over.
Your hand on my shoulder.
Remember the five and dime
The root beer floats
Remember my T-bird?
Window panes and
Prayer in schools and folks keeping their word.
I remember the glory days
Just like September,
I remember
Sweet sixteen and Ben Vereen.

I remember it all like September.
I remember the glory days
Frank Sinatra and big bands
Ray Charles Sonny and Cher
I remember it all just like September,
The way we were.

Beautiful Ladies

Irreplaceable, that's you.
Babies sing to you;
Gentlemen sing too.
Your song is on the radio.
Cafes copy your flavor.
Patients see you like flowers.
Churches depend on you.
The world thrives because of you.
You hold us up in the air
Above the fray.
You save the way!
It's a beautiful day
Only you can do what you do.
The world is beautiful because of you,
All of you are special, unique, irreplaceable, desired by kings.
You are beautiful from inside out.
Every fiber of you reveals what you are all about.
Walk proud with confidence.
You are gentle, you speak soft, not loud.
Ladies, you are the meaning of beautiful, the queen;
That's what you are.

Natural

I take off my wig and wear my natural.
No makeup, just passion.
No designers, just what God lends me.
I am fashion, culture, taste, and class.
Naturally me, naturally me.

God made me beautiful and free to be the real me.
I don't have to straighten, tuck, or airbrush.
I am natural; body and soul. I AM NATURAL.

TV isn't real life.
I love what God gave me.
Every bit, every part; natural from the very start.
Natural like the soil, plants, and fruit.
So natural, like the skin I'm in . . . I AM NATURAL!

Tell it Like it Is

Tell the truth.
Let the chips fall where they may.
Let go of lies and deceit today.

The truth will prevail,
Where lies will fail.
It will cleanse your inner spirit.

Let the truth set you free!
Holding onto lies causes pain and misery.

Remember, if you tell one lie,
It will lead you to tell another and another
Which can cause much trouble.
Let it go; forgive yourself.
And you will begin to forgive others.

Tell it! Let the chips fall where they may.
Don't live with useless lies, not another day.

Telling the truth will relieve your mind,
Freedom and peace, you will find.
Tell it like it is.
What will be, will be.
So let the truth set you free.

Special Eyes

Warriors change their eyes for special ones.
They see beauty in a grain of sand.
Clench infinity in one hand.
Capture the essence of nature at dawn.
See heaven and angels.
Fluorescent streets and grand parades
Hear jubilation and serenades.

Sing, "We shall overcome."
With special eyes, they see Malcolm
And Martin shaking hands.
These eyes are extraordinary.
Mahalia appears; singing unity.
Clench infinity!
Find serenity!
Get you a pair,
If you dare!

PLEASE
HELP!

Homelessness

A job lost after many years' hard labor;
Turns into picking up cans and bottles.
Turns into cold hard pavement and turns a mind inside out.

That man pushing a cart looks like me.
His hair is messed up, but he and I favor.
He digs in the trash for food.
He's at Broadway and Fifth,
Waiting for me to turn any corner.
Cup in one hand, he motions to me.
The blessing I imparted is temporary comfort.
At night, I often pray that he will see better days.

Look at Me

Look at me . . . tell me what you see!
I'm more than just a pretty face
What about the rest of me
Look at me! Well, I'm just like you
Looking for something to do
I'm going to the office too
Mortgage is due.

Look at me
Don't push past me
Or ignore my advice
You can be nice
After all we are neighbors
I don't need no palm reader
I'm no bottom feeder
Look deeper and you will see the real me
Then, we both will be free.

SECTION 4

Spiritual

The God in Me

You look at me and wonder why I smile and feel so free
I'll tell you why, it's the God in me
He is the reason I have the victory
I'll shout, I'll stomp my feet,
I'll dance up and down the street
For it's the God in me

Let's shout, let's dance, spread the word all over God's land
Let's dance, let's prance, till the power of God comes down
Let's join hands in unity, let's give praise for victory
Let's give praise for the God in me

Sinner's Prayer

Hey God, I want to pray, but don't know how.
Hey, I need to get this weight off me!
I know you can help me.
Don't forsake me like I did you.
I don't know what else to do.
I've been through every door.
And my feet and hands hurt.
I can't do this anymore!
I admit that I am a sinner,
That you are the way.
Is this how I should pray?
I need you today.

Bent Not Broken

I steal. I sell. I stall.
My faith, God keeps me.
Bent not broken,

God has spoken,
Bent out of shape, but reshaped.
Bent is gone, I move I mend.
Now I know, I can do all things through Christ . . .
I win, I work, bent not broken.
True words are spoken.
Today, I'm bent on my knees,
Thanking God
For victory!

An Angel at My Side

I have an angel at my side,
Better than any bodyguard.

I have an angel by my side.
I'm so thankful all my needs are supplied.
Thank you, Lord for the angel's guide!

No matter what the world is saying.
Have faith in God and keep on praying.

I have joy in the Lord and an angel at my side.
I feel the presence.
Like the warm summer breeze.
Touching my heart with ease.
Moves me, directs me.
I have an angel by my side.

I feel the brush of wings opening.
Like the comfort of mother's arms
Always present, always there.
Angel at my side.

Listen, Listen

Listen to the whistling of the wind
Listen to the soft voice that dwells within
Listen to the beating of your heart
A chorus of sacred words culminating to a melody of song
Listen quietly you will hear the voice of God
Psssst . . . Listen, listen.

To You I Cling

I have no wings without you
No hope without you
Restore me, help me define me
To you I cling

The one who solves all woes
To you I cling
You are my everything
With you I'm free
I know this because you gave me eyes to see

To you I cling

Wings That Never Fail

My wings never fail they take you to the high place.
The king of glory gives me wings to find heaven.
What a friend that never lets you down.
My wings can beat the speed of sound.
I am pure heart and pure soul.
A woman who loves the Lord.
A soul that has travelled far.
My faith is spiritually driven.
My wings expand to the heavens
They are angelic sails; God is the wind beneath them
My wings never fail.

Who?

Who made the sun that shines so bright?
Who made the stars that glisten all night?
Who made the mountains so beautiful so high?
Nobody but my Lord
He gave the moon its light shining on my face
Who gives us mercy and everlasting grace?
Nobody but my Lord

Section 5

Inspirational

Hold Your Head Up, Child

Hold your head up, child; don't look down.
Hold your head up, child; turn your life around.
Hold your dreams tight and fly.
Hold yourself together, try!
Hold onto your mind and learn to achieve.
Hold back your urges and believe.

Hold your head up, you're beautiful.
Hold onto your life; be dutiful.
Hold yourself up when you get pushed down.
Don't walk around wearing a frown.
You're better than those cliques or crowds.
Hold your head up child!

Hold your head up child and pull your pants up.
Tell me again what's in your cup.
Don't chase those streets just for treats.
Don't participate or sign up for defeat.

Hold your head up child
And you'll be able to see for miles.
Learn how to love starting with you.
That's the key to your wealth.

Hold your head up, child!
Hold your head up, child!
Don't look down.

Stepping High

Stepping high, high stepping.
Stepping up for love.
I'm stepping out of pain.
Twelve stepping.
Giant steps like Coltrane.
Listen up,
Steps ahead.
Sidestepping trouble, man!
Stepping high, high stepping.
One step up,
One step down.
Stepping all over God's land.
Stepping high, high stepping.
Stepping in.

Call Me a Pioneer

Don't call me a senior citizen,
Call me a pioneer.
You might as well cheer!
I've opened more doors than you have closed.
Like the Queen of England and Aunt Rose.

Don't say I should retire
Don't push me aside
And take my things.
Don't treat me like Rodney King.

Don't plan my trip to heaven;
I might be going to Greece!
Don't put me in a home
Or leave me all alone
I fought for this country;
What have you done?
I am not the one!

Don't call me a second class
Citizen or decommissioned.
I'll always have a position.
I make the world go around too!
Come sit and learn from me;
One day, grandma and grandpa
Will be free!

I Am Woman

With aspirations and dreams,
Spirited, I'll be free.
With redemption,
I am gold.
My story is pain and triumph.
I can fly.
I survive like the wolf.
Many try to belittle me, but I grow stronger.
I'll be free in love.
I'm honey made by many bees.
I'll be free to love,
Built, to be a woman and not die for my looks
Or my body.
I'll be free!
I am WOMAN!
Capital W-O-M-A-N!
The first lady of earth.
Mistress of advice
My words are gold.
My story is pain,
Come see me again.

I give birth to freedom.
I'm honey made by many bees.
I am good like dim sum.
I believe in love and the dove.
I am woman, I hurt like you.
My heart has been broken into tiny pieces
And landed on the island of "Survivor."

My life has purpose.
I am you; are you me?
I am woman. I am your dream.
I build things while I sleep.
But when I awake thousands of books I see.
No ceiling to stop me,
Only the cosmos.

Stand Up

All young men,
Don't sit down when others steal your right to live.
Stand up for your rights like all the brave did.
Stand your ground, isn't a right to kill.
Another life is claimed.
Who can we blame?

My fellow citizens stand up for your rights.
We're losing our youth right in our sight.
Stand up!
Let's stand together
Instead of killing one another.
Stand up!
Take a lesson from the wise.
Remember God is on our side.
Stand Up!!

Words

Like dancing on my tongue,
Words reach out and touch.
They can feel real good
Or really bad, I mean bad.
In the heart and mind words are born to live,
To grow and become teachers,
Healers, and priests.
They are like the songs of Bessie Smith.
They run like Jessie Owens,
They hit like Serena Williams.
They unfold like tulips,
They can float like a butterfly and sting like a bee.

Words beat inside of a soul like drums.
Splatters like a dropped dish.

The word was with God in the beginning.
Folks twist words and spit lies like a poisonous snake
Killing the love words create.
Words are meant to be angelic, to fly, and to soar.

Words can make bitter sweet love possible.
They are offsprings of newfound glory.
They are magical, majestic, and passionate.
They won't be quieted,
They won't shut down.
They won't be defeated!
Words are born to live.

So Much

So much to say and no one to listen.
So much love to give.
So much loneliness, but I'm not alone
I still got faith in God
So much hope.

I Am

I am not ashamed of who I am.
I am magnifying grace.
I am renewed spirit
I am the blind faith of hope
I bring, love, peace, and harmony.
Didn't I tell you, I am spirit!
You cannot catch me unless you love me.

I am victory!
I can reach anyone or any place.
I am not ashamed of who I am.
I am uplifting the meek.
I am elevating to higher heights.
I am like a solar plane of hope.
Can you see where I am coming from?

Station to station, heart to heart
Did I tell you I am like a solar plane?
You can't catch my flight unless you love me.

History Made

Opportunity American!
Gettysburg or Selma. Take your pick.
Barack Obama or Nelson Mandela.
Barack is number 44.
History made.
Opportunity American!

Martin Luther King Jr. has tears in his eyes.
Tears in his eyes.
Rosa Park has tears.
God's own hand designs these tears,
This opportunity to restore, to unify,
To love, to build, and to bear doves.
Opportunity America!
Some Americans shed tears of sorrow and rage.
Democracy must not be slayed.
Barack Obama . . . history made.

Tell the Truth

Tell the truth
Let the chips fall or fly
Lose the lies
The truth shall prevail whereas lies shall fail

Tell one lie, it will lead to another
This can leave one and all smothered
Tell it! And let the chips fly
Don't live with a useless lie
Tell the truth; free the mind
Give sight to the blind

A Change Starts with You

A change starts with you and me
How will you handle it?
A change just dialed your number
Check your mail
The young watch and wonder
While the old chase snails

A change starts with you
It can help you stay afloat
You must offer to do more than row your boat
A change comes to better you and me
"Brother can you spare some change"
Can we exchange the gift of change?

Section 6

Romance

Missing You

The warmth of your touch travels through me.
The wetness of your lips bathe me
I am captivated by your orbit,
By your stars
Your endless arms are all through me and around me.
You and I are one celestial world.
When you are not here I can feel what I've been missing
Lonely nights abound
When you're not around
Don't ever put me down.
Come back here and reverse this frown
I'm missing you

Don't ever put me down
We belong to the same kingdom
And it is magical
Isn't love wonderful?
Please stay with me
Hey, come back!

What Happened?

What happened to our love?
Did it fall sadly into the flowing water?
Did it burn up in an uncontrollable fire?
We are like pigeons wandering off
Because the bread is gone.
Our sweet tea has lost its sweetness.

What happened to our love?
Did it break down on the highway?
Did it catch the wrong flight?
Since we are still breathing, let's
See if you and I can share a breath.

What happened to our vows?
We are like old news footage;
We don't get pulled up.

What happened to our dreams?
They became nightmares
And custody battles.
I get the dog!
We both get the shaft.

What happened?

Must Love Tree

I pray to God for this love to grow
Like roots into the soil
Like the solid foundation of a great oak
These arms are meant to hold you
Like a must love tree

I long for beautiful gardens when I'm in your nature
Like butterflies I seek to the nectars of the soul
Thereby I will obtain that which must be preserved

Like harmony to a song
Like lovers do the tango
I pray to God I never lose this blissful glee
For therein I must find my must-love tree

Soul to Soul

Listen to the rhythm of our heartbeats
A synchronized melody so soft and sweet
These beats plunge us into pillow land

Two hearts flying together like birds of a feather
Forever one love, one mind body and soul
One heart beating as one, soul to soul

Here Comes the Holidays

Here comes the holidays.
The streets and pots are brimming.
I love feasts with all the trimmings.
Santa is ringing his bell.
Gifts are pouring like the rain.
Lights are going up from pane to pane.
Happiness is a new scarf and a full belly.
Online shoppers are on the telly.
The mail lady is on the move.
Cars can hardly move.
Here come the holidays!

Dear Santa

I want Daddy to come home.
I want Mama's back not to hurt.
I want Mama to get a big kiss and hug.
I know that you can answer my request
Because you aren't make-believe. Wait a minute!

You are really the Lord.
You are glory.
I love you, Santa; I mean Lord.
Where you are, it's not cold,
It's always sunny.
Instead of reindeers, you have angels.
Instead of one day a year,
You have always been forever.

This is a small request
Because you aren't make-believe.
But wait a minute!
I know my Santa is really my Lord.
You don't wear a red suit.
You wore a beautiful flowing purple robe.
I loved Santa as a child, but now I've grown dear Lord.

My Xmas Stocking is Rocking

My Xmas stocking is rocking to the beat of love, peace, and praise
Uplifting Jesus name throughout the holidays
My Xmas stocking is rocking for children everywhere
Bringing love and happiness wherever there is despair
My Xmas stocking is wider and longer this year
Because it's overflowing with gratitude and uplifting cheer

My stocking runneth over with love overflowing
For little children everywhere with starry eyes glowing
For the peace of God is in me as long as I am breathing
My Xmas stocking will forever be the reason for the season

I'll Be Your Fireplace

I'll be your fireplace, warm your days.

I'll be your stocking suffer for the holidays.

Let's light this house up with cheer

And get ready for Santa and his reindeers

Let's take off all our cares because love

And happiness is in the air.

Santa Claus won't be coming down the chimney

He'll be coming down the stairs.

Holiday gift giving starts now so just be prepared

To be a warm fireplace and have holiday cheer,

To eat and make merriment for the New Year.

I'll be your Fireplace to warm your sweet home.

I'll be your great love and never leave you alone.

I'll be your Fireplace to warm your heart

That way we will never be apart.

I am Woman

I am Woman
Capital W-o-m-a-n!
Your Condoleezza Rice
Master of advice
I am gold.
My story is pain
And starring roles.
Mother Teresa, Evita,
Ann Frank
I give birth to freedom.
I'm honey made by many bees
I am good like Dim Sum
I believe in love
And the dove.
I am Woman, I hurt like you.
I feel rejection and pain like you.
My heart breaks like yours.
Tiny pieces landed on an island called "Survivor."
My life has purpose.
I can't be voted off the island.
I am you; are you mine?

Roses for Me

A dozen roses arrived at my door, a surprise to some.
It never happened before.
I'm enjoying their beauty more than you know.
I've waited and anticipated for them to show.
I'm not waiting anymore for a guy and I'll tell you why . . .
I love me, I adore me.
By the way, the roses are from me.

Love Miles Away

Love lasted for years never sealed.
It caught a flight and stayed away.
Love miles away.

No more fights or sleepless nights.
No more walking on eggshells.
No more sweet-bitter rites.
Love miles away.

The distance is moon-like.
Love miles away.
No more sweet-bitter pill.
I'm doing just fine, for I have peace of mind.

I value my alone time.
Love at best, miles away.
The distance between us saved the day,
Love miles away.

Raindrops

I'm listening to the raindrops falling on my roof top,
Each drop intensifying my longing for you.
The sound of the rain is like an aphrodisiac,

Memories, so many memories.
Rain, go away, let me see a sunny day.
So many days and nights I've longed for you.
Hearing the sound of your footsteps,
Listening for the sound of your car pulling into the driveway.
Each time, my heart skipped a beat
Missing your touch and body heat.

Rain, go away!
Let me see a sunny day.

Love, Peace and Sweet Tea

I don't want coffee with sugar and cream
I want Love, Peace and Sweet Tea
Don't want a house on a hill with bills
I want Love, Peace and Sweet Tea
Don't want a man with slick dreams
I want that sweet, sweet Tea

Swirl me some honey!
Brew me baby! Brew me!
I need hot waters of love
Teas of peace soothe me sometime!
Move me! Shake me up!
It tastes so good on my plate
Savor the flavor, savor the flavor
It takes my mind to the blissful side
Pour honey all over me
Put it on me, I want passion
Give me the Sweet Tea
Honey baby fill me up
That's all I'm asking
Let's blend together
Let's drink sweet tea
I want passion on my palate
I want Love, Peace and Sweet Tea

Love Lost

The love lost because of wrong.
Because of things taken
The love lost in a storm.
Car accident, to cancer
JFK Jr. in a plane
Sweet woman to a train
The lost to an explosion
Twin Towers or Twin Peaks
Get out your lair!
The lost children crying
The lost homes
Romeo falls into a deep
stupor.
Cupid folds.

I Am Civilization

I Am Civilization, African Diaspora.
My breast have fed the world.
My legs have open up equality
I Am humanity, I Am Ms. Pearls.

I keep my bible near,
I keep my bible close.
I light the world. I light the world.
The ones who love the most
Light the world!

I plant the seeds and they grow.
Cook the meals and they eat.
I Angela Davis my days.
When do I get any sleep?

Working overtime to get by
Or asleep in the bleachers:
I Am Civilization, Nzinga,
Oprah Winfrey feature.

Apples pies, peach cobbler
I Am *love*, Peace, and sweet tea!
I wash and I scrub.
Who really loves me?

I light the world. I light the world.
I – light – the – world.

Super Woman

My love is powerful it makes me a Superwoman.
I heal with my love. I feel so blessed!
I can lift this world above my head.
I can fly above my own stress.

Ladies! We are all Superwomen!
Let your super life shine!
Hey Superwoman! Where is your cape?
Hey Superwoman; it's your time!

If my man can't love my superhero life
I'll flyaway, away.
Only God can really use me.
I'm especially super when I pray.

My love is powerful it makes me a Superwoman.
I trust in real love from above.
Hey ladies! Let your Superwoman rise.
Rise with the Dove.

I'm a Superwoman!

Serenity at Dawn

Open up to the real you
Get *off* the couch
I'm over the sad posts
Come out of your kangaroo pouch!
Hey Picasso!

How about serenity at Dawn
Strawberries and Cream
Sweet tea of life
And a slice of American Dream

Loose a few pounds for you
Love peace and sweet tea!
Go find your thing to do
Ain't it time to be free?

I'm in love with you, some me!

Face Off

The thoughts of You breaks
into my dreams
And kill the sheep.
A hockey puck would die
in our power play
We face *off*.

If I were Ovechkin
I'd teach you a lesson.
I can score more goals
Than you think.

We face *off*.

If I were a Blackhawk
Or Penguin I'd play
You in a playoff
And take away the cup.
We love to face off.
Take that face off.

Love is Worth It

Love is worth taking the risk, for a true love relationship & bliss
The excitement of my racing heart gives me hope for a brand new
start.
Love is worth it all a chance, for a brand new beginning, is worth
it all.
Love is worth is all
True Love is worth taking a risk, for that special someone,
sharing a mutual love,
Joy, and respect is worth it all!

Empress of the Fringes

Empress of the Fringes

A bag lady you say. Mattie isn't a bag lady; she's empress to the fringes. Mama and family don't want Mattie—only the corners, alleys, and empty fields want a drinking woman. Her drinking put disharmony in her household and sent Mattie to the streets. The woman keeps a bottle of Black Plague. She hangs around Leimert Park area because this is the last known address of the elementary school her two children attended. Mattie eats out of the dumpster and at local community food houses, where she frequents these familiar places.

Girl, Mattie once managed a children's clothing store on King Boulevard. The lady had it goin' on. She sewed most of the clothing people were wearing back then. She had customers from all over the city and even shipped her wear to the islands. Her husband was from Ghana, a medical student when she met him. What happened, you might ask? Hold on, don't rush! I'll get to that part, the juicy. To continue, Mattie has been on the streets since 2001. She ran away from home at the age of forty-two.

She is well known by the LAPD who used to run ol' Mattie from in front of beauty shops, wig shops, and grocery stores. Once people got to know Mattie, all the fuss ended. Mattie is Empress of the Fringes and more importantly, ambassador of the Western Hemisphere. So she says. Mattie doesn't ask for money; people just give her cash and fine clothing. She sometimes questions her loyal subjects being that they acknowledge her status as Empress of the Fringes.

Mattie removes her blanket from her face to reveal sunken eyes, dried tears, matted hair blackened by hard earth. She seems to rise as Mattie is about to speak as if a mic and lectern are before her. She asks, "Is God real? Does He really live up there?" Mr. Seals, the security guard at the A1 Cannabis Club, says the most in response. "God is real. He woke ya up this mornin', didn't he?" That man starts moving like a younger fellow at this point. He always does his thing the same way. I wonder if all the stuff that Mattie sees and does is part of a recurring theme park or loop that certain people are on.

"Mattie Love didn't think I knew your name. I remember you. You was a dressy thang. Up here talkin' 'bout is God real. You are His evidence. I look at how you sleep on that bus bench on Vernon in front of the park, and I say to myself, that woman is a surviving queen of a group that just got took out. I mean wiped out by crack, violence, and poisons. Don't you have a family? You do, I bet you do!"

"Okay! I ran away. Left my babies and their daddy twice. I couldn't . . . I couldn't stop drinking; then someone started in on me. They won't get out of my head. I tried to be back with my kids, but it didn't work. I hit the ceiling. I wanna run right now!" Mr. Seals and Mattie talk at least once a day. Mattie goes to Skid Row to eat and wash up during the day and return to the Leimert area in the evening. That is Mattie's routine. She used to go to the airport and watch the planes come and go, but her hearing got to where she couldn't handle the noise. Now, her permanent places are still in Leimert, and she frequents Los Angeles' downtown Skid Row. "Whoop! There it is!"

Oh, the voices start when Mattie drinks from her secret bottle. They cry at first then the voices get angry. Mattie shuts down when the voices come. The voices come when she reaches Skid Row. "Mattie Jean Love!" "We know you Mrs. Business." "You plan on opening another store? Ha ha ha." Mattie covers her ears and shakes her head until the voices turn whispers. The voices have ghostly fume. Mattie can see the faces behind the voices. They are mean, old, and ugly. The voices are from another time. Sometimes the voices are heard from other people. When they are in people, watch out! They are dangerous! "Go tell ya mama I said it!" Old Man Barnes goes on a tear in Gladys Park in Skid Row. Barnes is one of the lost souls. Two of the lost souls from Skid Row had been sleeping on the 40-Line, which Mattie often rides to and fro.

Once, Barnes and Mattie got into a throwing fight on Fifth and Crocker. Mattie had stashed some belongings—coats, flashlights, socks, and records. Old Man Barnes found the stash at nightfall and took what he wanted—ten records, mostly James Brown and BT Express. Mattie went to war until she found out it was Barnes. Mattie had this walk like a stately person.

Old Man Barnes ran when he saw Mattie. She caught Barnes throwing cans and old food parts until he surrendered. Old Man Barnes pulled a knife. Mattie hit him with a big stick, and he ran over to Gladys to hide. Mattie got along with most, but Old Man Barnes was a foe from the start. He cut lines and broke windows to fix on heroin. He mixed it with medication. Mattie, being bipolar, knew what was up with most of the Skid Row folks. She knew the woman the cops shot last year. The cops almost jumped Mattie over dumping her things two months ago. Barnes hates Mattie. He wants to cut her in her sleep. Problem, he can't figure out where she sleeps at night.

Paul, the preacher crossed paths with Mattie in Downtown Skid Row. Paul couldn't hide his disgust for the stench and neat filth in Mattie's Skid Row stomp. Paul wanted Mattie in the church. He believed that she had a calling in music ministry. That's how he first met Mattie: singing. Mattie was singing to herself, some James Brown. Paul was singing, "This Little Light of Mine." They bumped into one another. Mattie, being empress and all, shouldn't live like this, but this was what she wanted. No one wanted homelessness for Mattie. She left her husband and kids, and never went back. Paul didn't dwell on those facts; he just wanted Mattie to know God.

"I know God is up there," Mattie laughed. "He got hell for me." Paul shook his head and reached for his Bible. Mattie started singing, "I Got the Feeling," as loud as she could. Paul wasn't deterred. He read quotes from the book of James. "I'm an Empress!" Mattie rant on about how royal she was. Paul agreed that she was royal. He kneeled and prayed before Mattie. Mattie found the praying stuff to be regal indeed. She fancied prayer more than singing because it really stopped the voices. The voices were no match for prayer or singing. This prayer thing just might have saved her family, she thought. It is better than alcohol and medication. Mattie made up her mind to go to church with Paul.

At the Church of New Hope, Mattie fell to her knees and asked God to forgive her. She tore her pink dress, the one a beautician had given her a week ago. It was a new dress with tags on it. Paul kneeled beside Mattie. Several other women came up in tears after Mattie raised her arms in surrender. Mattie cried, trying to hold back her pain. Years came out. Years of pain flowed through like Katrina's Storm. Mattie opened her eyes, a brightness, which made the ceiling lights appear dim and in need of changing.

The voices showed Old Man Barnes where Mattie slept—Leimert Park. Barnes took some change and boarded the 40-line. "I want you to be a man again," the voices cried. Barnes listened with his bloodshot eyes and spoke with his yellow teeth. Barnes wanted to fly to Crenshaw, but no planes landed there. For Old Man Barnes believed in Lucifer. He felt Mattie was out to hurt his master. He wanted the Queen of Skid Row, the Empress of the Fringes to eat dirt.

When Old Man Barnes arrived on Crenshaw, two others met him. They didn't speak only pointed southward in the direction of Leimert Park. Mattie was singing James Brown, "It's a Man's World," Old Man Barnes was at the light staring. Mattie hadn't noticed the three foes. She was calm like a gentle sea. Mattie got under her covers on what was a cold and misty night.

The moon stood bright in the sky. Barnes waited until Mattie fell asleep, then he eased over behind the bench as the other two foes served as lookouts. He pulled out a large blade and looked to see if the woman on the bench was indeed Mattie. Once he saw it was the empress, he aimed his blade, but his hand could not plunge the blade. He couldn't move. Mr. Seal and several park regulars had grabbed Old Man Barnes and his two accomplices and pulled them away from Mattie.

The cops came and took Old Man Barnes to jail for having a knife in his hand in the middle of traffic. The other two foes ran away in the blackness. Mr. Seal took Mattie to a hotel by the airport. "No! Don't pay for a room!" Mr. Seal slept in his grey Ford truck to make sure Mattie was safe. Mr. Seal's license plate read, "God is Real."

LAPD alerted Mattie of an old missing person's report posted with her name and photo on it the following morning. Contact information was in the file; detective gave Mattie her family's new number since they moved out of Leimert Park some years ago.

Two days later, Mattie got to see her son and daughter, Gary and Natalie. Mr. Seals drove Mattie to live in her new home, which her husband purchased before his sudden passing, legally Mattie was still married because neither she nor her husband filed for divorce. Her children, Gary and Natalie, now adults were overjoyed to see their mom for the first time in thirteen years. "Mama, we prayed you would come back home, where have you been?"